PRAYER CONQUERS

STRUGGLES

AND

DISAPOINTMENT

By

Nilsa V. Brown, Ed, D

ISBN-13: 978-0989907200

ACKNOWLEDGEMENT

This is my first book and I want to express gratitude to my mother Cosma Hunter Brown, because I am what I am because you love me, to my children Franjehi J. Morgan and Sharleen S. Morgan these two youngsters saw me experience misfortune, pain, and struggle, but because I lived by the word of our Lord Jesus Christ He subsequently blessed us all with **HIS** generosity and distinct ability to transform each one of those hurts, and challenges in to triumph.

When I began to birth this book my inspiration came from the steadfast confidence that I have in our Lord Jesus Christ, and my father, Ralph Brown who passed away nine years ago; I miss him so much because he was my spiritual strength. Thanks to three special persons who regularly lend an ear to listen to my burdens and worries and positively opened their hearts to me in a unique way.

Writing this book has been a grand pleasure because our God Almighty guided me through the entire process. To experience closeness with our God is beyond measure.

Because of the closeness that I experienced with our God Almighty while I was in the process of birthing this book I bequest this book to every person. This book is a powerful example of transformation and growth in Christ.

Our Heavenly Father is a wonderful and Loving Friend who can always be at your side to help, comfort and cheer you up. Just talk to **Thee** in a meek and trusting way. Our Dear Father always delivers miracles our highest good. He doesn't grant desires; God makes reality works.

Whenever you are experiencing struggles and disappointment trust God and wait patiently. God will suddenly lift you out of darkness into a brilliant sunlight. Please remember God is never late he is always on time.

Contents

PREFACE

It is imperative for every person to understand the need to pray every day. Christians from all walks of life and every level of society are struggling to acquire the discipline to pray, they have utilized manuscripts, handbooks, electronic resources, and participated in prayer seminars; hence a vast majority of Christians continue to slip back due to stronghold from nuisance from diverse sources which have kept them from experiencing the glory and power that a life of prayer can provide.

I was raised in a Catholic family setting and I lived the difficulties that my parents experienced with one of my siblings; a **brother**, Satan unlocked every tactic he had on his life. My parents did not recognize the battlefield, so no strategies were put in place to effectively win the mêlée against Satan.

On the contrary as an active member of the 700 Club The Christian Broadcasting Network, one of the longest running Christian based television programs I knew that difficulties are placed in our lives in order to develop character in our souls and that battles are not fought without the help of God, so when I got married and became pregnant, and then learned that I was going to conceive a boy; without apprehension or fretfulness I immediately humbled myself and visited with our **Heavenly Father** I placed myself under the Cross of Jesus Christ covered myself with His precious Blood surrounded myself with the light of Christ, subsequently I was able to place the armor of God and my un-borne child today he is an educator and a man of truthfulness is name is Franjehi.
Years after when I learned that I had conceived another child, a baby girl, I then humbly sought His work to be accomplished in her life. Once more Jesus Christ answered my plea.

iii

Today my daughter has grown up, and have acquired a master's degree in Educational Leadership and is a young woman who's passionate and full of love for our **Heavenly Father**. I pray every day that my two children daily walk will remain deeply rooted in our Heavenly Father and expand exceedingly.

Harshly in 1992 right after *__HURRICANE ANDREW__* the enemy of God knocked on my door and unknowingly I let *Him* in; soon after I began to confront adverse circumstances, overpowering obstacles, discouragement, ending resources, test and trials, it almost felt like the Lions' Den. (Daniel 6: 16-23) but since I was wholeheartedly committed to God my faith was firm and immovable God rescued me and saw me through I was not defeated. It is my desire that everyone that has an opportunity to enjoy this book will begin to develop a lifelong relationship with the greatest friend one could ever know. **Jesus Christ.**

What Is Prayer?

Prayer is a basic form of interaction that effectively connects population to God a spiritual consciousness in which we tie ourselves in to a relationship with God until we are part of his plan and his purpose.

Prayer can additionally be stretched over in various other ways as petition for others, which is known as intercession. If we have faith of the size of a mustard seed one can receive "whatever" we ask for in prayer. Matthew 21: 21, 22. Remember God wants you through prayer to be the kind of person **He** elected for you to be when he placed you on this earth for the first time.

What Do We Pray?

We have to pray concerning others and ourselves and who are bound by spiritual bondage and are spellbound in manacles and chain up. Populations ought to pray and not faint build up strength and go forth in power and authority and take the enemies' camp by storm. Remember God said to don't look back; at the rear of you is former times, although former times is what brought you to now, it is not what will take you into the future. God is the rewarded of those who diligently seek and serve HIM.

Why Do We Pray?

A Christian prays because prayer is the antidote to fretfulness it alleviates our weariness; it deepens our relationship with God. By way of prayer, we are transformed and renewed prayer reminds us that we are dependent on God and not on ourselves. For Jesus said, "Ask and it will be given to you; seek and you will find; knock and the door will be opened to you." (Matthew 7:7). God is able to do immeasurably more than all we ask or imagine, according to his power that is at work within us.

Who Should Pray?

Prayer is vital and essential to all. God instructions to us are do it all the time. We often should give up sleep and food at times in order to pray more and with full power. Christians ought to look to the Holy Spirit to help us to pray effectively and give us the right words with which we can pray.

When Do We Pray?

It is important for Christians to develop a habit of prayer according to one's faith and desire. There are no rigorous commands as to what time and in what way one should pray. Prayer should be a regular, repeated part of our daily lives; we should never give up or cease the practice of prayer. Further, we should live so that we are always ready to pray at any moment.

The (7) Seven Steps to Prayer

Prayer has no specific procedure, but basic positive elements should be included in our contact with God and these are: Adoration, Confession, Examination, Forgiveness, Surrender, Supplication, and Thanksgiving, (ACEFSST).

- Adoration

- Confession

- Examination

- Forgiveness

- Surrender

- Supplication

- Thanksgiving

Adoration

Is the strict sense, an act of religion offered to God in acknowledgment of his supreme perfection and dominion, Is an interior act of mind and will; the mind perceives that God's perfection is infinite, and the will bidding us to extol and worship **HIS** perfection.

Confession

Is the opportunity we have to pursue God and to talk about one's deep concerns, It is believed that no intermediary is necessary between the Christian and God in order to be absolved from sins. Psalm 51 is a confessional prayer.

Examination

Christians should examine themselves at the place of their new beginning, or their new start, as well as right through their future life to see if they are truly born again. This comes by way of examination of the Christian's faith, and believes.

Forgiveness

Confess your sins to the Lord Jesus Christ and ask for HIS forgiveness. Announce that you forgive all persons who have done you wrong. Verbalize their names as you confess that you forgive them.

Surrender

It is the will to be submitted to Jesus. It brings you to a position of weakness before Him. It is important to learn to say yes to Jesus with all of your heart and soul and to believe and trust that is objective is being labored in each situation, and circumstance, according to our extent of readiness.

Supplication

This is the time when persons goes to God and asks **Him** in a modest and trusting manner to meet their needs. Practice asking for each thing or need through the day anywhere you are. "Ask and it will be given to you; seek and you will find; knock and the door will be open to you."

Thanksgiving

This is the time when you become specific in thanking God. Example, Thank YOU, God for empowering me each day, Thank YOU God for eyes to see Thank YOU God for ears to ear, Thank YOU God, for my employment, Thank YOU God for my children, Thank YOU God for giving me favor with YOU, Thank YOU God for freedom from sickness. Amen!

Praying with the Psalms

The psalms are a rich resource of prayers it introduces us to a dialogue with God. The prayer of the citizens of Israel has been the psalms. The psalms have been written over a period of approximately eight hundred years.

The book of psalms consists of five books, which are separated, in this style.

The psalms have been the song and prayers that was used by Jesus, Mary, the Apostles, and Jews, and are still prayed daily by millions. Use the list below to guide you in your daily prayers. Make it your personal prayer book.

Book	Psalms
1	1- 41
2	42 – 72
3	73 – 89
4	90 -106
5	107 -150

Need	Psalm	Verse
Confidence	115	11
	62	8-9
	40	1-5
	37	3-5
	32	10
	40	1-5
	56	4
	25	10
Conversation	130	4-8
	80	18-20
	65	3-4
	51	
	32	
	25	
Family	147	13
	133	
	132	12-16
	128	1-6
	112	1-9
	89	31-34
Fear	91	
	71	
	49	6
	34	
	27	
	23	
	18	

God	148	
	147	
	111	
	104	
	93	
	89	
	24	
	23	
	19	
	8	
Growth	146	
	119	9
	115	
	78	
	41	
	36	
	18	29
Health	147	3-4
	107	17-20
	103	2-4
	90	7
	41	2-5
	38	
	34	19
	30	

Messiah	132	
	118	22
	110	
	45	
	21	
Petition	102	
	70	
	69	
	56	
	55	
	49	
	43	
	38	
	32	
	22	
	7	
	5	
Praise	150	
	149	
	148	
	146	
	135	
	113	
	89	

Salvation	95	1-6
	80	4-8
	62	2-8
	50	23
	37	39
	27	
Security	90	
	86	
	71	
	61	5-6
	56	12
	46	2-4
	17	6-7
	16	
Strength	118	
	71	3-5
	46	2-4
	28	7-9
	18	32
Thanksgiving	138	
	136	
	118	
	116	
	103	
	86	
	66	
	34	

Chapter 1

Day After Day Prayers

PRESENT YOURSELF

TO the Lord

IN PRAYERS

PETITIONS

AND FULL

Gratitude

THE EYES OF THE LORD

Are On The

Righteous,

And His Ears Are Open to

Their Cry

Psalm 34:15

CRACK OF DAWN

Dear Lord

Thank **YOU** for this new day

Thank YOU for been the light in my life

I am surrendering to **YOUR**

Guidance and Protection

I humbly ask for **YOU** to cover me with

Your blood and anointing

Make clear my path

Protect me from

All evildoers and evil forces

Grant me

Health work and favor

Dear Lord

Bring happiness

To my home, family, friends and peace on earth

Goodwill towards all men and women

Amen!

(The Lord's Prayer (2) twice

EXALT

(Bless)

Dear Lord

I am feeling **YOUR** presence

Right here

Your love surrounds my life

Thank **YOU** for teaching me

Love, patient, joy unselfishness, faith and serenity

Dear Lord

By faith I know that **YOU** are always there,

Thank **YOU** for teaching me

To live, and move only by faith

Dear Lord

I am

Strong and secure in **YOU**

Preserve me

For in **YOU**

I put my trust

Amen!

STRENGTH

Lord

YOU have never fall short

To be a vital and warm friend

Please grant me

A new consignment

New-inspired brain

A new light

On my future

Keep me strong

Place my life

In the center

Of **YOUR** will

Shape me in to the person **YOU** want me

To be

I am willing waiting listening

Sustain my move in **YOUR** path

Amen!

REPENTANCE

Dear God

My spirit, soul and body are humble

I am weeping out to Thee

My heart is weighed down

Be merciful to me

Dear God

Forgive my transgression

Purge me with hyssop

Make me clean

Sanctify me with a clean heart

Bless me with a new and right spirit

Raise me up

My heart is overwhelmed

Guide me to the **rock** that is higher than I

Psalm 61:2

Amen!

Hyssop: biblical plant

PROTECTION

God of my salvation

Protect me from the snare of the fowler

Save me from all impurities

Help me to stand

Firm against

The Devil's tactics

And crush <u>HIM</u> under my feet

God of my salvation

Stand guard over my heart and mind

Keep me in a safe place

YOU are my shield

My strong defense against **evil forces**

Under your wings I am safe

Amen!

Chapter 2

Beyond
Our
Control

Have Mercy upon Me

O God

According to Your

Loving Kindness;

According to the Multitude Of

Your Tender Mercies

Blot Out My Transgressions

Psalm 51:1

UNSPOKEN

Loving God,

I lowly come before **YOU**

To surrender my misery affliction and shortcomings unto **YOU**

(Unspoken...)

Loving God help me

Remove this_____ from my heart

Pull me out of the pit

I trust **YOU** to restore me

To lead me from pain to peace

I know **YOU** want my **highest** good

Lead me by **YOUR** spirit

Teach me to live one day at a time

Enlighten me so that

I will not meddle in what is beyond my power

Loving God

I am leaning on **YOU** unconditionally

Please do not forsake me

Amen!

REQUEST

Heavenly Father

Rewarded of the meek

I give myself to **YOUR** armor

Be my guardian always

Take this mug of suffering from me

Yet **YOUR** will Dear God; not my will

Heavenly Father

You are bigger than any trouble challenging me

Right now

I hand over all my needs spiritual and earthly to **YOU**

Guide me in the way of devotion and salvation

Make my mind holy

That in all things it may

Be enlightened by faith

I place myself beneath the cross of Jesus Christ

I want **YOUR** power in my life

Please fill me now Lord.

Amen!

TRUST

Dear Lord

I bring my doubts, perplexities, and temptations to **YOU**

In **YOU**, O Lord I put my

Trust let me never be ashamed

Psalm 31:1

You are a righteous God save me, I pray

Lord in hours of loneliness, weariness, and trials

Help me I pray

When my heart is cast down by failure,

Help me I pray

When I feel impatient, and my cross irritates me

I begged for **YOUR** help Lord

When I cast myself on your tender Love as a Father and Savior

Help me Lord

Dear God **YOU** are my refuge and defense

Shelter me from danger

Guide me and lead me as **YOU** have promised

Psalm 31:3 -5

Amen!

DELIVERANCE

Dear God

I am dreadfully (roughly) hurt

Saturate me with conviction

To know that **YOU** are with me

Facing me, next to me, in me, beneath me and over me

Dear God

Give me a new mind

To accept whatever is brought before me

Even when there's a storm

To remain calm

You are my light

I wait for **YOU** Lord

Renew my strength,

Mount me up with wings like eagles

Let me run and not be weary

Walk and not quit

(Is 40:31)

Amen!

SURRENDER

Dear Lord

Attend to my cry

I have forsaken you and rejected **YOU**

For a very long time I am here face down

Before your altar I am yours

And yours I wish to be

Look in to my eyes the eyes of my heart

I am hungry for YOUR love be merciful to me

I am **tarnished** by sin

Dear Lord

I THIRST FOR **YOU**

Console me strengthen me

Lift me up and bind all my wounds

Dispel all darkness, burdens and doubts be my light

With **YOUR** power and grace touch my heart

With your peace still my soul

And transform my life

Amen!

Chapter 3

Livelihood

Power

If you have faith **as**

A grain of a Mustard seed,

You shall say

Unto This Mountain Remove

From Here

To There and It Will move

And Nothing Shall Be

Impossible Unto You

Mathew 17: 20

ARMOR OF GOD

O Lord my God I am standing firm

With belt of truth buckled around my waist

My feet is fitted in place with the shield of faith

And the helmet of salvation O Lord my God, in **YOU** I put my trust

Save me from the powers of the dark world

Protect me against the spiritual forces of evil

Ephesians 6:12

Save me from all those who persecute me

And deliver me keep me from the traps

That they have put down for me

And from the traps of the workers of iniquity

O Lord you save those who trust **YOU**

From those who rise up against them

Keep me as the apple of **YOUR** eye

Hide me under the shadow of **YOUR** wings,

From the wicked who oppresses

O God; Thank **YOU** for **YOUR** mercy

Amen!

GUIDANCE

Dear God

I lift up my spirit to **YOU** O Lord

Reveal your ways to me direct me in **YOUR** pathway

Show me the way of **YOUR** truth

I have faith in **YOU**

Dear O God,

Give ear to my supplications

Do not remember the sins of my youth nor my transgressions

According to **YOUR** mercy remember me,

For **YOUR** goodness sake, O God,

Psalm 25: 7

Do not hide **YOUR** self from my supplication

Attend to me and ear me, O God

Psalms 55:1, 2

I will hum praises to **YOU**

Guide me and deliver me, O God!

Amen!

GRACE

Heavenly Father

I throw myself on my knees

Before **YOU**

And with burning desire

I plea and implore to **YOU**

Stir upon in my heart

Spirited sentiments of trust, hope and kindness

Guide me in the repentance

Of my knowingly wrong doing

Enable me to have resolved desire of change

Heavenly Father,

Strengthen me

Sanctify and save me

I place my trust in **YOU**

Glory and honor unto **YOU** forever

Amen!

CONFIDENCE

The Lord the most high is awesome

He leads me in a smooth path

My feet is upon a high rock He is my joy, strength, and salvation

My heart shall not fear

O Lord **YOUR** justice is like a large mountaintop

Though evildoers shall rise up against me

They shall stumble and fall

God of my salvation In **YOU**, I put my trust

Be my fortress and defense

Cover me with **YOUR** blood and anointing

Guide each and everything I do each day

O God

My heart, body and soul are fixed on **YOU**

I am standing on **YOUR** word

Because **YOUR** word never fails

Amen!

FAITH

Jesus

Epitome of truth, image of harmony wholeheartedly

I surrender my whole being to **YOU**

To be used for righteous purposes

I will pray to **YOU** persistently

No matter what trials or tribulations comes my way

I will live or die for **YOU**

The joy of the Lord is my strength

John 10:10

There is no problem unsolvable for God

No fear is unconquerable for **YOU**

My faith in **YOU** Lord is unshakable

It will not be silence or quench

There is power in Jesus name

I will never quit

I will receive what I ask from God thy will not my will

Halleluiah!

Chapter 4

IN TIMES

OF

SORROW

Dear Jesus

Give me strength NOW THAT I

am

Broken down and deserted

Take Care of Me This Day

Help Me Believe In Your Love

and CARE

And That You Are Going To

Guide My Healing

I Trust In You

Nilsa Brown, Ed, D.

SUDDEN LOSS

Dear God

I am face down with sorrow

My life is suddenly distraught in to pieces

I am overcome by uncertainty and confusion

The road before me looks dark

Dear God

I am committing myself to **YOU** I surrender my grief and sadness

Come to my assistance please comfort me

I need to be close to **YOU** in praise and worship

Take care of me each day

Lord I exalt **YOUR** holy name **YOU** are the almighty God

You are the all-powerful omnipotent

Lord of Heaven and earth

I surrender my sorrow to **YOU**

Be merciful to me O God

For I cry to **YOU** all day long

I give you full power over my life

Amen!

OVERWHELM

Heavenly Father

I am weeping and sobbing crush with grief

Feeling helpless and lonely

I believe I have reached the end

Please, please empower me

To deal with my loss courageously

Lead me out of despair and pain soften this taste of grief

Help me to understand that

Every end leads to a new beginning

When my father and mother forsake me

The Lord will lift me up

Sorrow never leaves **YOU** where it found **YOU**

Weeping may endure for a night

But joy comes in the morning

Psalm 30:5

Thank **YOU** Lord Jesus

Amen!

EMPTY

Sorrow, grief weighed down my hearth

I am racked with pain and heart broken

The mystery of loss of life tackles my mind

Fearful and empty I stand with my loss

Heavenly **FATHER** fortify my soul

Help me find a way to cease this pain

Fill my heart with renew hope

Heavenly **FATHER**

Build my spiritual character

I trust **YOU** minute by minute

Provide me with a ray of sunshine

Healing and peace to my hearth

Amen!

RENEWAL

Christ the anointed one

Today I come before **YOU** with a petition

Filter my thoughts and the purposes of my heart

Renew and transform my mind

Fix my mental power

And what is pure and worthy of reverence

Father I incline my ear unto godly wisdom and instruction

Dear Lord

My delight and desires are in **YOUR** law

I will walk in the path of uprightness

When I walk my steps shall not be hampered

My path will be clear and open

I shall not stumble

Halleluiah!

COMFORT

God Almighty

I am thankful to **YOU** for been my stronghold

Who is able to understand and sympathizes with

My grief and loss over

_____

I humble my self

Before **YOUR**

Altar of mercifulness

Console me and give me strength

Lift me up carry me, touch my heart

Give me consolation and hope

Lift me out of the shadows of sorrow

Help me deal with this loss boldly

You are my heavenly father

My faith is in **YOU**, my helper

I trust in **YOU**

To heal my pain

Amen!

SADDEN

Loving God

Draw me close to **YOU** today

I am suffering right now

Spare me from further pain

Remove anxiety from my heart

Comfort me in my sorrow

Sustain me by **YOUR** power

Console me by **YOUR** love

Fill me with joy

Because Death is a lead up to rebirth

I am depending and **YOU** to restore me

Dear God

Amen!

Chapter 5

Warfare

Our Struggle Is Not

Against Flesh

And Blood,

But Against

The Rulers

Against The Authorities, Against

the Powers

Of This Dark World

And Against the Spiritual

Forces of Evil in the

Heavenly Realms

Ephesians 6:12

POWER

Dear Jesus, I come before **YOU**

In worship and glorification

YOU are my energy, my hope

Empower me each day give me courage and wisdom

To recognize the dangerous sharpness of evil in all forms

Protect me under **YOUR** wings

In the name of Jesus Christ

And His precious blood

I bind every demonic spirit

From any source from injuring me in any way

Precious Jesus **YOUR** love is constant

Surround me with **YOUR** light

Thank **YOU** Lord, for watching over me

In Jesus name

Amen!

LIGHT

Dear Lord

These minutes belongs to **YOU**

Things are going wrong the strong man is at work

I am pull down despondent and depressed

Funds are low the debts are like a mountain

(_____personal_____)

Dear Lord

Do something beautiful in my

Spirit, and in my soul today

Set me free from the power of evil

By **YOUR** power, and presence

Dear Lord

I am depending on **YOU** to move the mountain

My faith is as small as a mustard seed

Nothing is impossible for **YOU** Lord

I am holding on to **YOU**

Let your light shine on me

Amen!

RELIANCE

Dear God **YOU** are my strength

My rock, my fortress my deliverer

I will not be afraid of any weapons, or trials, that

Forms or comes up against me

I rebuke Satan I set my self under

The cross of Jesus Christ

I mask my body with His blood I carry God's shield

To defy the Devil's plans

I bind all forces of Evil In the name of Jesus Christ

God is with **ME** in times of trouble

He will rescue me His spirit of confidence lives in my heart

With Him I cannot fail

If God is for me who can be against me

Dear God **YOU** are the guard

Of all who places

Their trust in **YOU**

Amen!

COURAGE

Dear Lord!

Release **ME** from bondage of anxiety, fears, worries, and guilt

(Personal request)

I no longer want to be enslaved

My heart, body, and soul are in **YOUR** hands

Make **ME** strong

Give me spirit of courage

To face the future courageously

Let **YOUR** peace which surpasses

All understanding bring **ME**

Tranquility and assurance

Thank **YOU** God

Amen!

WORSHIP

I adore You, Jesus;	You are the Light of the World
I adore You, Jesus;	You are the way for my life
I adore You Jesus;	You are my hiding place
I adore You, Jesus;	You are all that I want
I adore You Jesus;	You are symbol of Peace
I adore You, Jesus;	You are the Rock of all Ages
I adore You Jesus;	You are the Alpha and the Omega
I adore You, Jesus;	You are the only truth
I adore You, Jesus;	You are the Almighty
I adore You, Jesus;	You are my life, my love
I adore You, Jesus;	(_____)

Continue with praise for as long as you want or need

My Dear Jesus

From deep within my heart I am so glad YOU are with me

I thank YOU for guidance nearness always

Thank YOU for YOUR wondrous power Thank YOU for being the

beginning and the end thank YOU for YOUR patience thank YOU for been

my provider

Thank YOU for my family thank for my children thank YOU for peace

Amen!

Chapter 6

SUPPLEMENTARY
PRAYERS

HOUSE PRAYER

Dear Lord I ( ) come to **YOU** with gratitude and admiration

I am (   ) grateful for this home

I plead the blood of Jesus on every door, ceiling, walls, windows,

And floors of this home

Holy Spirit **YOU** are welcome in this home and in my life

Fill this home with **YOUR** presence

Let me feel **YOUR** presence

Let peace, discernment, harmony, solidarity and love bound this home

Dear Lord I trust this home to **YOU** today

Raise it up on a solid **ROCK**

Keep evildoers and spirit away from this home

Dear Lord I humbly ask for **YOUR** blessing each day

When I depart from this home

Dear Lord Pilot my vehicle

Please be beside **ME**, before **ME**, behind, below **ME**, above **ME**

Deliver me to my destination safely and return me back safely

Ruler of my heart please never part from **ME**

Amen!

TRAVELERS PRAYER

Father of love and power,

I am on a Journey today far from home

Guard me from danger

From confound, disturbance, fire and foe,

Through this world of toil and snares

Protect me wherever I may go

Guide my feet hold my hand

Please keep me from all wrong

I am **YOUR** child

Stay with me while I am on my way

Keep light and hope in my heart

Fill my life with love, joy and peace

Because of **YOUR** mercy I shall rise to Thee

I will sing and shout hymns of praises

Thank you **FATHER**

Amen!

JOURNEY

Dear God, YOU are my light

Today please grant **ME** YOUR precious gifts

To strengthen and guide me on life's way…

Help **ME** meet the opportunities of this day

With optimism and courage

Please restrain **ME**

When temptation comes way

Dear God

Fill **ME** with

Understanding and discernment

To do things **YOUR** way

Please be with **ME**

Dearly respected light

And hear each plea I speak.

Amen!

HOLY SPIRIT

Holy Spirit

YOU keep everything transparent for **ME**

YOU light up my path way

So that I can accomplish all my needs

YOU give **ME** the divine power to pardon and put

Behind **ME**

All the wrong that has been done to **ME**

YOU are with **ME** every moment of my life

Holy Spirit

I want to thank **YOU** and confirm once more

That I never want to be separated from **YOU**

No matter how great my pertinent illusion could be

My desire is to be with **YOU** and my love ones

In everlasting praise

Thank **YOU** for kindness

Amen!

THE OUR FATHER

Our Father, who art in Heaven

Hallowed be thy name

Thy kingdom comes

Thy will be done on earth

As it is in heaven

Give us this day our daily bread;

And forgive us our trespasses

As we forgive those

Who trespass against us

And lead us not into temptation

But deliver us from evil

Amen!

THE HAIL MARY

Hail Mary, full of grace

The Lord is with us

Blessed are **YOU** among women,

And blessed is the fruit

Of **YOUR** womb, Jesus

Holy Mary, Mother of God

Pray for us sinners,

Now and at the hour of our death

Amen!

THE APOSTLE'S CREED

I believe in God, the Father Almighty

Creator of heaven and earth

I believe in Jesus Christ, his only Son, Our Lord

He was conceived by the power of the

Holy Spirit,

And born of the Virgin Mary

He suffered under Pontius Pilate,

Was crucified, died and was buried

He descended to the dead

On the third day He rose again

He ascended into heaven,

And his seated at the right hand of the Father

He will come again to judge the

Living and dead

I believe in the Holy Spirit

The forgiveness of sins, the resurrection

Of the body and the life everlasting

Amen!

TIME OF NEED

Dear Lord

I come before **YOU** this day

I bring this special need

_____

Lord I am depending on **YOU** no one is greater than **YOU**

I trust in **YOU** Dear Lord

Lead everything in my best will

My hope is in **YOU** Lord

You are my help and my shield

I am still, patient and waiting on **YOU** Lord

Surround me with **YOUR** unfailing love

O Lord my Savior do not forsake me

YOU are my help and my rescuer

An eternally present help in trouble

Help me at the break of first light

Thank **YOU** Dear Lord

Amen!

DEDICATION

Dear God

Your faithfulness reaches the sky

My heart is steadfast (firm)

I will give thanks to **YOU**

Halleluiah!

Even when

I am at my worst

I will

Continue

To have

Burning sentiments

Of faith and hope

In my hearth

Because **YOU** love **ME**

Halleluiah!

ABOUT THE AUTHOR

Dr. Nilsa V. Brown was born and raised in Colon, Republic of Panama, and currently resides in Miami, Florida. Dr. Brown is certified by the Florida Department of Education in Mathematics and English for Speakers of other Languages. Her natural ability is education and she has done so for more than 25 years worldwide for various public school systems.

Equally, she edified at the higher education level for Florida International University and at Miami Dade College. Her services in education have been classroom teacher, school planning and management, team discipline coordinator, Mathematics Department Leader, Administrative Assistant, and Mathematics Educational Specialist for Miami-Dade County Public Schools Division of Mathematics and Science Education.
Additionally, she coordinated the (ESOL) English for Speakers of Other Languages Program for the Title One Program at Campbell Drive Elementary School in 1995. She wrote several grants to improve Mathematics learning in the classroom for middle schools. She is a PROJECT VISION Teacher and Trainer since April 1999. The Dade County Council of Teachers of Mathematics nominated her Mathematics Teacher of the Year in the year 2000.

Dr. Brown Educational Accomplishments are: A Bachelor's Degree (BA) in Business Administration and Accounting from the University of Panama, a Master's Degree (MA) in English For Speakers of Other Languages from Nova University in Fort Lauderdale Florida, an Educational Specialist Degree (Ed. S) in Mathematics from Florida State University in Tallahassee Florida and an Educational Leadership Degree (Ed. D) from Nova Southeastern University in Fort Lauderdale, Florida.

In 1992, after *HURRICANE ANDREW*, she experienced extensive personal loss, injustice, and the prowl of the enemy, Satan. She prayed for guidance, watched and waited until one day, Our God Almighty, wrapped His arms around her tightly and inhaled strength back into her weary body. She then learned that no one needs to bear pain; all we need to do is bring everything to God in prayer who can lead us from defeat to *VICTORY*.

www.ingramcontent.com/pod-product-compliance
Lightning Source LLC
Chambersburg PA
CBHW031934080426
42734CB00007B/685